CONTEMPORARY
PIANO

12 FAVORITES
ARRANGED FOR SOLO PIANO
BY STAN PETHEL

MODERATE DIFFICULTY

Lillenas Publishing Co.
KANSAS CITY, MO. 64141

CONTENTS

How Majestic Is Your Name

with Holy, Holy, Holy

MICHAEL W. SMITH
Arr. by Stan Pethel

Smoothly
*"Holy, Holy, Holy"
(John B. Dykes)

decresc.

mf

When Answers Aren't Enough

SCOTT WESLEY BROWN
and GREG NELSON
Arr. by Stan Pethel

Only Jesus / Calvary's Love

GREG NELSON and PHILL McHUGH
Arr. by Stan Pethel

Freely, with expression
*"Only Jesus"

*"Calvary's Love"

Great Is the Lord

MICHAEL W. SMITH
and DEBORAH D. SMITH
Arr. by Stan Pethel

People Need the Lord

GREG NELSON and PHILL McHUGH
Arr. by Stan Pethel

O Magnify the Lord

DICK and MELODY TUNNEY
Arr. by Stan Pethel

Moderately fast "classical feel"

Lamb of Glory

GREG NELSON and PHILL McHUGH
Arr. by Stan Pethel

More Than Wonderful

LANNY WOLFE
Arr. by Stan Pethel

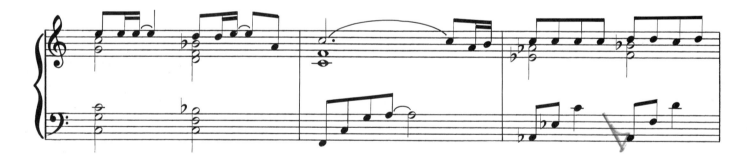

Via Dolorosa

BILLY SPRAGUE and NILES BOROP
Arr. by Stan Pethel

Proclaim the Glory of the Lord

NILES BOROP and DWIGHT LILES
Arr. by Stan Pethel